Joseph Banks

Heidi Moore

www.heinemann.co.uk/library
Visit our website to find out more information about **Heinemann** books.

To order:
☎ Phone 44 (0) 1865 888112
🗎 Send a fax to 44 (0) 1865 314091
🖥 Visit the Heinemann Bookshop at **www.heinemann.co.uk/library** to browse our catalogue and order online.

Heinemann Library is an imprint of Pearson Education Limited, a company incorporated in England and Wales having its registered office at Edinburgh Gate, Harlow, Essex, CM20 2JE – Registered company number: 00872828

Edited by Louise Galpine, Rachel Howells, and Adam Miller
Designed by Kimberly R. Miracle and Betsy Wernert
Original illustrations © Pearson Education Limited
Illustrations by Mapping Specialists, Inc.
Picture research by Mica Brancic and Helen Reilly
Originated by Modern Age
Printed and bound in China by Leo Paper Group

ISBN 978 0 431 04479 8 (hardback)
13 12 11 10 09
10 9 8 7 6 5 4 3 2 1

British Library Cataloguing in Publication Data
Moore, Heidi, 1976-
Joseph Banks. – (Levelled biographies)
508'.092
A full catalogue record for this book is available from the British Library.

Acknowledgements
We would like to thank the following for permission to reproduce photographs: © Air Club Villa p. **41**; ©Alamy p. **19** (The Print Collector); © Corbis pp. **9** (Stapleton Collection), **10** (Skyscan), **12** (Raymond Gehman), **13** (Bettmann), **23** (Tony Aruzza), **24** (Atlantide Phototravel/ Guido Cozzi), **27** (Franz Lanting), **35** (Steven Vidler/ Eurasia); © John Arron p. **7**; © NASA p.**18**; © Natural History Museum, London pp. **4**, **14**, **17** (Loten Collection), **29**, **37**, **39**; © Reuters p. **21** (David Gray); © The Bridgeman Art Library pp. **16** (Linnean Society, London, UK), **34** (Lincolnshire County Council, Usher Gallery, Lincoln, UK), **33** (Private Collection, © Agnew's, London, UK), **36** (Private Collection, Ken Welsh); © The National Library of Australia pp. **20**, **22**, **26**, **30**, **40**; © The National Portrait Gallery p. **31** (William Parry); University of Massachusetts Library p. **38**.

Cover photograph of Joseph Banks reproduced with permission of © Bridgeman.

We would like to thank Nancy Harris for her invaluable help in the preparation of this book.

Every effort has been made to contact copyright holders of any material reproduced in this book. Any omissions will be rectified in subsequent printings if notice is given to the publisher.

CONTENTS

Some words are shown in bold, **like this**. You can find out what they mean by looking in the glossary.

NATURALIST AND EXPLORER

Joseph Banks lived from the mid-18th to early 19th century.

Sir Joseph Banks was a famous British explorer and **naturalist**. A naturalist is a person who studies nature. He lived from 1743 to 1820. Banks had a strong interest in **botany**, which is the study of plants. This led him to travel around the world. His travels took him to faraway places such as New Zealand, Australia, and Tahiti. On these voyages, he discovered many new **species** (types) of plants.

Spreading the word

During his life, Banks went on only three major voyages. However, they proved to be very important. On these trips, Banks saw hundreds of plants and animals that few people in Europe knew of at the time. Everywhere he went, he took careful notes about what he saw. He also gathered many samples. This way he could share what he had learned after he returned to England.

Later, important scientists from all over the world wrote letters to Banks. Many visited his home in London. They all wanted to see Banks' huge plant collection. It was filled with thousands of samples that he had collected on his voyages. Banks opened up this collection to anyone who wished to see it.

Sir Joseph Banks changed science forever. He went on important voyages, he made careful **observations**, and he was willing to share what he learned with others. Banks' findings shaped the course of botany. He gave us greater knowledge of the natural world.

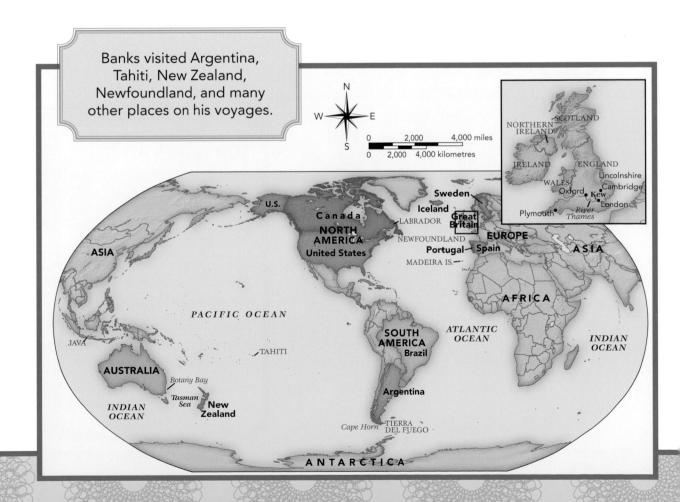

Banks visited Argentina, Tahiti, New Zealand, Newfoundland, and many other places on his voyages.

An English gentleman

On 13 February 1743, an English woman called Sarah Banks gave birth to a son. She and her husband, William, named the boy Joseph.

Joseph Banks was born into a wealthy family. Many people in London knew of the Banks family. A monthly newspaper even printed news of Joseph's birth! It only printed news of seven other births that month. This shows that people thought the Banks family was important.

Joseph's father, William Banks, was a barrister. A barrister is a lawyer who appears in court. William Banks also served as a Member of Parliament. Parliament is part of the government that makes laws.

Young Joseph grew up on the family's country estate. It was called Revesby. Revesby was in Lincolnshire. It was a large piece of land near the coast. The estate had a large house and 138 hectares (340 acres) of land. Wild deer roamed the estate. There were stables with horses to ride. Joseph spent lots of time outdoors. He loved fishing in the lake.

Warts and all

As a boy, Joseph Banks shocked his friends by rubbing toads on his face! He did this to prove that toads did not cause warts. Many people believed this at the time. Banks' mother had told him that toads were harmless.

Banks spent part of his childhood at Revesby estate. You can see it here, in the distance.

These trees, grown at Revesby, came from seedlings that Banks discovered on one of his voyages.

Off to school

In 1752 Joseph Banks left home to attend school. His parents sent him to Harrow School, just outside London. Harrow was a boys' **boarding school**. This means that the boys who went to the school also lived there.

Banks was only nine years old but he was not the youngest pupil at Harrow. Boys as young as five years old lived there on their own! Local women helped take care of the pupils when they were not in class.

At Harrow, Banks studied Latin and Greek. But he was not a dedicated pupil. He loved playing outside and found it hard to pay attention in class. His father was disturbed about this, and decided to send Banks to a different school. So, at age 13, he left Harrow.

Life at Harrow

Harrow is one of the most famous schools in England. Several former British prime ministers attended Harrow. The prime minister is the person who leads Britain. Many old Harrow **traditions** are still alive today. Pupils wear straw hats called boaters and call their teachers "beaks".

Learning Latin

Latin is a very old language. It is no longer spoken, but many people still learn it. The English language comes partly from Latin. Many science terms, such as plant names, are Latin. For example, the Latin name for sweet pea is *Lathyrus odorata*. Knowing Latin is helpful for the study of **botany**.

Joseph Banks did not stand out as a pupil at Harrow.

A budding botanist

In 1756 Joseph Banks began studying at Eton. Eton is another famous school in southern England. Banks did better at Eton. He finally learned to write Latin. By now he was 14 years old.

That year he found a subject that really held his interest – **botany**! One story says that Banks became interested in the subject while walking along the River Thames. He noticed the beautiful wildflowers along the river and decided he wanted to learn more about plants.

The River Thames flows through southern England.

Soon Banks began reading everything he could about plants. He also started collecting plant **specimens** (samples). He wanted to start a **herbarium** (plant collection).

Oxford University

In 1760 Banks went off to study at Oxford University. However, at the time it offered few science classes. Most pupils studied Latin and Greek. These subjects did not interest Banks. He paid a **professor** from Cambridge University to come to Oxford to teach him botany. The professor agreed! This way, Banks was able to continue learning about botany.

In 1761 his father unexpectedly died. Suddenly Banks was the **heir** to a fortune. At age 21 he would receive an income of £6,000 a year. That amount would not make him wealthy, but it was more than enough to live on. Now Banks did not have to worry about having enough money.

HIS FIRST ADVENTURE

In 1764 Joseph Banks turned 21 and **inherited** the fortune. He left Oxford without finishing his degree and bought a house in London.

In 1766 Banks received good news. A friend from Eton, Constantine John Phipps, was about to head out on a sea voyage. Phipps invited Banks to come with him. The ship, the HMS *Niger*, was to travel to Newfoundland and Labrador. Today, that area is part of Canada. Banks planned to collect plant **specimens** while he was there.

Newfoundland is an island off the Atlantic coast of Canada.

What's in a name?

Ship names often start with the letters "HMS". This stands for "her **majesty's** ship" or "his majesty's ship". "Her majesty" and "his majesty" are titles of respect for the queen or king. The ships were named this way because they sailed in the service of the king or queen who ruled at the time.

Banks saw many unique **species** of birds in Newfoundland and Labrador.

Banks was excited. Few people in the world had taken such a journey. The *Niger* set sail from Plymouth, England, on 22 April 1766. It took the ship about three weeks to cross the Atlantic Ocean. At first the weather was terrible. Banks was so seasick he could not even write!

Soon Banks felt well enough to write in his **diary**. He began to note every plant and animal the ship came across. His entry of 25 May 1766 reads: "Walked out today to gather the male blossoms of a plant resembling [looking like] Dutch myrtle, which grows in **bogs** and watery places."

Starting the collection

Banks had wanted to meet Inuit (native Newfoundland people) on the voyage, but that did not happen. Still, it was an adventure. In Newfoundland and Labrador he saw various new plant and animal **species**. He collected dozens of samples to bring home. On the way home, the HMS *Niger* sailed past huge icebergs.

This fish is one of several new species that Banks came across on his travels.

The ship finally returned to England in January 1767. It had spent nine long months at sea. The trip was a huge success! Banks brought back more than 340 plant **specimens** from North America. The ship carried 91 birds, many fish, and a few **mammals**. There was even a spiny porcupine on board.

Now Joseph Banks was a real **botanist**. He had gained skills in the field. While he was away, the Royal **Society** had elected him a fellow (member). This was a group of British scientists that had been founded in 1660. The group's aim was to promote science.

Banks now had one of the best plant collections in the world. This was the start of his famous **herbarium**.

Strange dish

Banks wrote in his **diary** about a new food he came across on his journey. French fishers living in Newfoundland ate a dish called chowder. It was a type of stew made from fish, salted pork, and diced potatoes. Banks thought it was a strange dish.

New adventures

It was now time for Banks to **classify** his collection. He began to group things by their **species**. He did this with help from another **naturalist**, Daniel Carl Solander. Solander soon became one of Banks' closest friends. Their partnership helped shape the future of **botany**.

Meet Solander

Daniel Carl Solander (right) was born in Sweden and lived from 1733 to 1782. He studied with the famous Swedish scientist Carl Linnaeus. Linnaeus was the founder of modern botany. In 1760 Solander moved to London. He taught people about Linnaeus's new system of classifying living things. Solander joined the Royal Society in 1764.

In late 1767 Banks travelled around southwest England and Wales. He met the Scottish painter Sydney Parkinson. Banks asked Parkinson to paint his **specimens** from the Newfoundland voyage. Banks would then have a permanent record of them. Remember, this was long before cameras!

In January 1768 Banks returned to London. He heard of a new voyage the Royal **Society** was planning. It was to be the first **scientific** voyage to the Pacific Ocean. Commander James Cook would lead the voyage. Cook was a master in the Royal Navy, and would become one of the most famous sea captains in history. However, not many people knew of him at the time.

The Royal Society asked Banks to go along on the voyage to record new plant species. Banks happily agreed!

Sydney Parkinson painted many of Banks' specimens, including this stork.

JOURNEY TO THE SOUTH PACIFIC

One reason for Banks' journey was to **observe** the **transit** of Venus. In the summer of 1769, the planet Venus was to pass across the Sun. The Royal **Society** thought it was important to have a group of sailors view it from the best point on Earth. That point was near the island of Tahiti, in the southern Pacific Ocean.

Viewing the transit of Venus would help scientists work out the distance between the Sun and Earth. This was very helpful for **navigation**. Knowing the exact placement of the planets and stars helped with navigation in the 18th century.

Another reason for the journey was to find the southern **continent**. Scientists at the time called this land *Terra Australis*. However, no one from Europe had ever been there. Some people doubted that there was such a place.

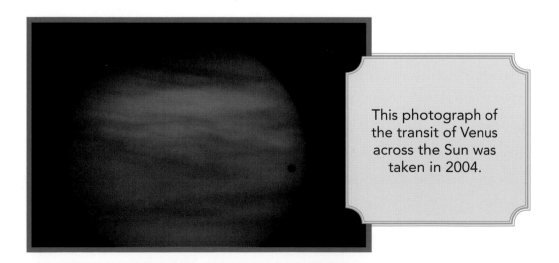

This photograph of the transit of Venus across the Sun was taken in 2004.

Meet Captain Cook

Captain James Cook (right) lived from 1728 to 1779. He was a British sailor and explorer. Like Banks, he went on a voyage to Newfoundland. He was the first to map that area. The first voyage he led was the voyage to the Pacific with Banks. The voyage would make him famous.

This painting depicts the HMB *Endeavour* off the coast of Australia.

Voyage of the *Endeavour*

Banks was now 25 years old. He was to serve as the ship's **botanist**. He brought seven men with him on the journey. One of them was his friend Daniel Carl Solander, the **naturalist**. Another was Sydney Parkinson, the Scottish artist who painted Banks' HMS *Niger* collection. Banks also brought four servants.

The group sailed on the HMB *Endeavour*. "HMB" stands for "his **majesty's** bark" or "her majesty's bark". A bark is a type of small ship with a flat bottom. It was not very fast, but it could sail smoothly in shallow water.

Captain Cook and his crew did not have the largest boat. But they had everything they needed. They had about £10,000 worth of tools and gear! This was a huge sum back then. Banks paid for all of it from the money he had **inherited**.

The *Endeavour* sailed from England on 26 August 1768. It carried 94 people, as well as Banks' two dogs, a cat, and a goat!

Endeavour's gear

John Ellis, a Member of Parliament, wrote a letter to the Swedish botanist Carl Linnaeus. The letter detailed what the *Endeavour* crew brought on board: "They have got a fine library of natural history; they have all sorts of machines for catching and preserving [keeping] insects . . . They even have a . . . telescope, by which, put into the water, you can see the bottom at a great depth, where it is clear."

A **replica** of the famous HMB *Endeavour* sits anchored in Botany Bay, Australia.

Life on board the ship

The ship's living area was small and cramped. Most of the crew shared the large main cabin. They slept above one another in small hammocks. Captain Cook shared his cabin with Banks, Solander, and Parkinson.

Just like in the earlier voyage, Banks was seasick at first. Soon, however, he was well enough to go on deck. He began writing down all the plant and animal life he saw. Throughout the voyage, Banks kept a detailed **diary**.

Banks' diary entry from 16 May 1768. In it he discusses a special soup called saloop, which was supposed to help with seasickness.

Banks' diary

"Calm today. Another insect, which we took today, was possest of [had] more beautiful colouring than anything in nature I have ever seen, . . . [except] gems."

Joseph Banks, 4 September 1768

The *Endeavour* first landed on the Madeira Islands, off the coast of Portugal, on 12 September. After just five days on shore, Banks had collected about 250 **specimens**. Gathering specimens took patience and courage. Banks had to leave the ship and explore the unknown land, looking for new plant **species**. Then, he had to carefully cut a sample to bring back to the ship.

Banks never knew exactly what he would find on shore. There could be danger. On the Madeira Islands, Banks discovered many exciting new plants. He took samples of bananas, pineapples, mangoes, guavas, and bark from cinnamon trees! (This is where the spice cinnamon comes from.)

Brightly coloured *Geum coccineum* flowers grow on the Madeira Islands.

Land of fire

In December the *Endeavour* headed south towards Cape Horn, the farthest point south in South America. In January 1769 the ship reached the tip of Argentina. The area is called Tierra del Fuego. This means "Land of Fire" in Spanish. The 16th-century explorer Ferdinand Magellan named the area after the bonfires he saw when he landed there.

Tierra del Fuego is a group of rugged, mountainous islands that belong to Argentina and Chile.

Banks, Solander, and other crew members went ashore for supplies. When they left it was calm and sunny, but suddenly the weather changed. It began to snow and they were forced to camp overnight. Two crew members froze to death on the trip. Banks and the rest made it back to the ship safely.

From there the ship headed west into the Pacific Ocean. Captain Cook sailed towards Tahiti.

Sailors' diet

No one on the *Endeavour* died of **scurvy**. Scurvy is a disease caused by a lack of vitamin C in one's diet. This was a common cause of death on long sea voyages in the 18th century. Captain Cook made sure his crew had a good diet. They ate watercress, sauerkraut, and plants they picked during the voyage. All these plants contain vitamin C.

Banks' diary

"Here is also plenty of wild celery [and] scurvy grass, both of which are as pleasant to the taste as any herbs of the kind found in Europe, and I believe possess as much virtue in curing the scurvy."

Jospeh Banks,
14 January 1769

THE SOUTHERN CONTINENT

The *Endeavour* spent three months docked near Tahiti. Banks gathered plant and animal **specimens** there. He also spent time with the people of Tahiti, learning about their way of life.

Later that year Captain Cook and his crew did what they came to do. On 3 June 1769, they **observed** the **transit** of Venus. Now it was off to search for the southern **continent**, the *Terra Australis*!

Unknown continent
Captain Cook did not find the *Terra Australis* on this journey. He believed there was a large, icy landmass farther south, closer to the South Pole. Later he discovered only the small continent of Antarctica. There was no *Terra Australis*.

This painting by John Hamilton Mortimer depicts Banks, Captain Cook, Lord Sandwich, and two others. It was painted around 1771.

A strange animal

Banks was one of the first Europeans to see a kangaroo! Banks wrote in his **diary** that it was "an animal as large as a greyhound, of a mouse colour, and very swift".

How would you describe a kangaroo to someone who has never seen one?

The HMB *Endeavour* sailed southwest from Tahiti. First, Captain Cook found and charted the coast of New Zealand. This took six months. Then, the ship crossed the Tasman Sea, heading west. On 19 April 1770, the crew spotted land. It was Australia!

The *Endeavour* sailed 3,200 kilometres (2,000 miles) along Australia's east coast. Along the way it made many landings. In April the ship dropped anchor at a bay that was especially good for finding specimens. Banks named it **Botany** Bay. Sydney Parkinson made 94 sketches of specimens there in just 14 days!

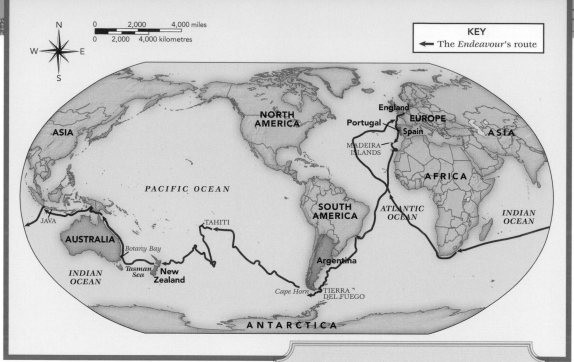

The HMB *Endeavour* circled the world on its three-year voyage.

Heading home

The HMB *Endeavour* sailed back towards England after spending nearly three years at sea. On the way the ship stopped in Java, an island in Southeast Asia. There the crew stocked up on rice, vegetables, fruit, sheep, hogs, and sugar.

By now Banks' plant collection was very large. The **specimens** were covered with wet cloths and stored in tin chests. This was how Banks kept the plants fresh.

In 1771 the ship returned to England. Everyone on board was treated like a hero, especially Banks. The voyage was a huge success! They had **circumnavigated** the world. They brought back a huge collection of plants and animals. In all there were about 1,300 new **species**.

Banks' and Solander's careful notes and Parkinson's drawings gave other **naturalists** plenty to study for years. The *Endeavour's* success also pleased King George III. The king was very interested in farming and **botany**. Many people called him "Farmer George".

Banks had seen more types of plant than any **botanist** before him. His success made people see the value of sending scientists on voyages of exploration. Now it was time to focus on his huge **herbarium**. No one in the world, naturalist or king, had as large a collection as Banks now did!

Sydney Parkinson drew this sketch. It is of some New Zealand warriors that Banks met.

FINAL VOYAGE

Soon Banks set about putting his collection in order. He stored it in his London home. This became his famous **herbarium**. In addition, one room held a huge insect collection and samples of about 3,000 plants. Another room held dozens of dead animal **specimens**. The same room held about 2,000 drawings by Sydney Parkinson.

Before long the Royal **Society** planned another trip. Lord Sandwich asked Banks and Cook to return to the Pacific Ocean. The HMS *Resolution* was to set sail in March 1772. Banks was not pleased with the ship. He thought the HMS *Resolution* was not large enough for his group.

The Royal Society may have planned their trips at dinners like this one. Joseph Banks is pictured on the right.

Banks told Lord Sandwich he would not go unless they made the ship larger. Lord Sandwich agreed. But on the ship's test run on the River Thames, it almost toppled over! It could not safely handle the extra weight, so the ship had to be adjusted back to its earlier size.

Banks was angry. However, the Royal Society would not give him a new ship. In May Banks removed his gear from the ship. He would not go on the voyage.

Visitor from Tahiti

Captain Cook returned to England in 1774 with a special guest. It was a Tahitian man named Omai. Cook and Banks had met Omai on the HMB *Endeavour* journey. Banks took his visitor all over London. Omai met many people before returning home.

This 1775 painting by William Parry shows Banks and Solander with Omai, the first Tahitian visitor to England.

Iceland

In 1772 Banks planned a voyage to Iceland. This was the last major voyage he would take. He chose Iceland because it was the closest place where he could still discover new **species**. Also, the journey there would not be difficult.

The *Sir Lawrence* set sail for Iceland on 12 July 1772. Banks brought most of the crew that was meant to go on the *Resolution*. His good friend Daniel Carl Solander, the **naturalist**, came with him. Sir William Hamilton, a member of the Royal **Society**, joined them as well. Hamilton wanted to study Iceland's volcanoes.

A disappointing trip

The ship arrived late in the year. By then it was too late to collect very much, as cold weather had set in. Banks and Solander were able to make only 14 plant drawings. However, they did manage to see the volcano and to climb on cooled lava flows.

On 18 October they set sail to return to England. The trip was nowhere near as successful as Banks' first two journeys. He did still manage to produce many **diary** entries about the country. He also brought back lava samples.

Home again

Banks was now 29 years old. He was ready to settle down in England. Banks never travelled around the world again. He now had many duties as a **botanist** and naturalist. He was still a member of the Royal Society. With the group, he helped plan and fund other people's sea voyages.

This image of Banks is from around 1771–1772.
He had sailed the world but was not yet 30!

SETTLING DOWN

In 1772 King George III took over his family's Royal **Botanic Gardens** at Kew. Kew is just outside London, on the banks of the River Thames.

The king knew of Banks because of the HMB *Endeavour* trip. He asked Banks for his views on what Kew should become. Banks thought Kew should be Britain's most important plant collection. It should house plants from around the world. The king agreed.

John Raphael Smith engraved this image of Banks in 1773.

Today Kew Gardens attracts more than a million visitors per year.

In 1773 King George made Banks the garden's director. That year Banks planted about 800 **species** of trees there. Many were from North America. Under Banks' guidance, Kew Gardens grew to become one of the most important gardens in the world. People from all over Britain visited Kew to see plants from around the world. There were **specimens** from across Europe, southern Africa, Australia, Newfoundland, and Labrador. Banks sent **naturalists** to many faraway places to gather yet more plants for Kew.

In 1774 Banks became a member of the Royal **Society's council**. The council was a group of 24 members who ran the society.

In 1776 Banks moved to a new house in London. The house was at 32 Soho Square. The Soho Square house had enough room for his huge library and **herbarium**. Scientists came from across Europe to view his collections.

Adviser to the king
King George sought Banks' advice about other things, such as sheep herding. Once Banks helped the king obtain several Spanish merino sheep. The sheep were prized for their fine wool.

Banks was 65 when this painting was made. He had been president of the Royal Society for 30 years.

Royal Society

In 1778 the president of the Royal **Society** stepped down. Many of Banks' friends urged him to run for president. Daniel Carl Solander was among them.

At 35 Banks was young to be president. However, people liked and respected him. After all, he was an adviser to the king. The Royal Society elected him president in December 1778. He later said that this was the greatest honour he ever received.

Banks held the position of president for the rest of his life. He was very active. He attended 417 of the 450 **council** meetings held in the 41 years he was president. He also sent and received many letters on behalf of the Royal Society. He once guessed that he wrote between 50,000 and 100,000 letters while living at Soho Square alone! Remember, this was before telephone and email. Writing was the main way people communicated with one another at that time.

Sir Joseph
In 1781 the king made Banks a **baronet**. Now he was called "Sir Joseph Banks".

Thirty-two Soho Square was the home and herbarium of Sir Joseph Banks.

The next year was a happy one as well. On 23 March 1779, Banks married Dorothea Hugessen. Joseph and Dorothea Banks had no children. They led a busy life in London. Banks still enjoyed the outdoor activities he had loved as a boy, such as hunting and fishing. He and his wife also had many visitors. **Naturalists** from all over the world came to view Banks' **herbarium** and library.

The *Florilegium*

Banks did not **publish** much work. He wrote only a few brief papers during his lifetime. His major work was to be the *Florilegium*. This would be a book based on his South Pacific journey with Captain Cook. The word *florilegium* is Latin for "flower-gathering".

It was a huge task to unpack, prepare, and put together information on the hundreds of **specimens** from the voyage. But by 1772 everything was ready. Banks' sister copied his South Pacific **diaries**. Daniel Carl Solander wrote the **scientific** descriptions.

Banks planned to publish a huge book. It would have detailed descriptions of the hundreds of plants he collected in Madeira, Brazil, Tierra del Fuego, New Zealand, Australia, and Java. It would contain 743 drawings based on Sydney Parkinson's paintings.

This is a sketch of the *Banksia littoralis* from Banks' *Florilegium*. This new **species** was named after Banks.

Old Man Banksia (*Banksia serrata*)
is also part of the *Florilegium*.

Banks worked on it steadily for about ten years. By 1782 it was nearly done. That year Banks wrote, "All that is left is so little that it can be completed in two months." But then nothing happened.

Perhaps he was afraid it would not be as good as he hoped. Then, in May 1782, his good friend Solander died. Banks loved his friend dearly. He may have been too upset to finish the project.

No one knows the true reason. But Banks' *Florilegium* was not published in full until 200 years after the voyage! The British Museum finally published the entire work in 1989.

LASTING INFLUENCE

In 1797 Banks was asked to join the privy **council**. This was a group of private advisers to the king.

Over time Banks' health grew worse. He suffered from **gout**. Gout is a painful disease that causes stiffness of the joints. He also gained lots of weight. He spent most of the last 15 years of his life in a wheelchair.

Joseph Banks left behind a large body of knowledge related to **botany**.

On 1 June 1820, Banks tried to step down as president of the Royal **Society**. The society would not let him retire, however. Just 18 days later, Banks died in London.

Joseph Banks was an important **botanist** and **naturalist**. He explored distant lands and brought back many new **species**. Banks' famous **herbarium** drew scientists from around the world. His collection of plant and animal **specimens** gave scientists enough samples to study for decades to come.

Banks' library supplied hundreds of important works on natural history. As the king's adviser, Banks helped Kew Gardens grow into one of the world's most amazing **botanic gardens**. He also urged people to settle in Australia.

Perhaps most importantly, Banks shared his knowledge with everyone. His house at 32 Soho Square in London was open to anyone who wanted to use his collection. He welcomed everyone, from humble gardeners to famous scientists. Banks may not have **published** much in his lifetime, but he found many other ways to share his knowledge!

The Banks Islands in the Pacific Ocean are named after Sir Joseph Banks.

TIMELINES

Joseph Banks' life

1743 Born on 13 February

1752 Leaves home to attend Harrow School

1760 Studies at Oxford University

1761 His father, William Banks, dies

1764 Turns 21 and **inherits** fortune

1766 Leaves on HMS *Niger* voyage on 22 April

Elected to Royal **Society**

1768 Sails from England on HMB *Endeavour* under Captain James Cook

1769 Ship reaches Tierra del Fuego in January

Observes transit of Venus in Tahiti on 3 June

1770 Reaches Australia on 19 April

1771 HMB *Endeavour* returns to England

1772 Sails to Iceland on the *Sir Lawrence* on 12 July

1773 Takes over as director of Kew Gardens

1774 Becomes member of Royal Society **Council**

1776 Moves to Soho Square, London

1778 Elected president of Royal Society in December

1779 Marries Dorothea Hugessen on 23 March

1781 Made **baronet**

1797 Admitted to privy council

1820 Dies in London on 19 June

World timeline

1738	Carl Linnaeus **publishes** major work, *Classes Plantarum* [Classes of Plants], which provides foundation of modern **botany**
1759	British Museum opens in London
1760	George III becomes king of England
1772–1775	Captain James Cook returns to Pacific Ocean, crosses Antarctic Circle
1778	Captain James Cook becomes first European to visit the Hawaiian Islands
1782	Swiss **botanist** Daniel Carl Solander dies
1793	The navigator Captain Bligh names group of volcanic islands in the Pacific the "Banks Islands"
1820	King George III dies
1989	British Museum publishes all of Banks' *Florilegium*
2003	Royal **Botanic Gardens** at Kew named a UNESCO World Heritage Site. This means that the gardens are a protected area with important cultural value.

Glossary

baronet title of honour given to a man that means he can call himself "Sir"

boarding school school where pupils live. Banks was only nine years old when he went to boarding school.

bog wet, spongy ground. Many plants can be found in bogs.

botanic garden garden where plants are cared for, studied, and put on display. The Royal Botanic Gardens at Kew feature a wide variety of plants.

botanist person who studies plants

botany study of plant life. Botany is the branch of science that deals with plants.

circumnavigate travel in a circle. The HMB *Endeavour* circumnavigated the world.

classify put into groups

continent large landmass. Antarctica was the seventh continent to be discovered.

council group that meets to give advice. Banks was elected to the privy council, which advised the king.

diary record of daily life. Banks kept a diary with details about his travels.

gout painful disease causing stiffness of the joints. Late in life, Banks suffered from gout.

heir person who is set to receive money, land, or other property from a parent. Banks was heir to his father's fortune.

herbarium collection of dried plant samples. Scientists came from all over the world to see Banks' herbarium.

inherit receive from a parent or ancestor. Banks inherited a fortune from his father.

majesty term of honour for a queen or king. His majesty's boat *Endeavour* sailed to New Zealand.

mammal furry, warm-blooded animal that feeds its young milk from its body. Humans are mammals.

naturalist person who studies nature

navigation act of working out a ship's position based on the stars and planets and moving from one place to another. Sailors in the 18th century relied on navigation.

observation information gained by watching. Banks' careful observations told him a lot about the natural world.

observe watch or look at something closely

professor university teacher

publish print information in a book or paper for lots of people to read

replica exact copy of something

scientific having to do with science. Banks made many scientific discoveries.

scurvy disease caused by lack of vitamin C in one's diet. Sailors often got scurvy, but no one on Captain Cook's trip to the Pacific died from it.

society group of experts on a subject. The Royal Society wanted to promote science.

species group of plants or animals that can successfully reproduce. Banks discovered many new species on his voyages.

specimen sample. Banks collected many plant specimens.

tradition belief or custom passed down over many years

transit movement. The transit of Venus took place when the planet moved across the Sun. It has happened only three times since Banks observed it in 1769, but is due to happen again in 2012!

WANT TO KNOW MORE?

Books

Great Journeys Across Earth: Captain Cook's Pacific Explorations, Jane Bingham (Heinemann Library, 2008)

Hobby Guide: The Young Naturalist, A. Mitchell (Usborne Books, 2008)

Kids' Kew: A Children's Guide, Miranda MacQuitty (Royal Botanic Gardens, 2007)

Websites

www.nhm.ac.uk
Look at the website for the Natural History Museum. Learn about different plants from the parts of the world Joseph Banks visited.

www.bbc.co.uk/history/historic_figures
Click on "B" and then "Sir Joseph Banks" to learn more about him. There are also pages on other well-known naturalists such as Charles Darwin.

www2.sl.nsw.gov.au/banks/banks.cfm
This site gives information about Sir Joseph Banks, including his role with the early settlements in New South Wales, Australia.

Places to visit

The British Museum

Great Russell Street • London WC1B 3DG • 020 7323 8000

www.britishmuseum.org

View drawings and engravings from Joseph Banks' plant collection as well as artefacts from Captain Cook's voyages.

The Royal Botanic Gardens, Kew

Richmond • Surrey TW9 3AB • 020 8332 5655

www.kew.org

Explore 121 hectares (300 acres) of plants and trees from around the world.

Revesby Estate

Revesby • Boston • Lincolnshire PE22 7NB • 01507 568 395

http://revesbyestate.co.uk

Tour Joseph Banks' childhood home. You can see some of the trees he brought back from his voyages.

INDEX